Text by Denise Jarrett-Macauley
Photography by Peter Barry
Designed by Philip Clucas
Produced by Ted Smart and Gerald Hughes
Editorial Direction by David Gibbon

CLB 1133
Copyright © 1985 Illustrations and text by Colour Library Books Ltd.
This edition published in the U.S.A. 1985
by Exeter Books.
Distributed by Bookthrift.
Exeter is a trademark of Simon & Schuster, Inc.
Bookthrift is a registered trademark of Simon & Schuster, Inc.
New York, New York.
Printed and bound in Barcelona, Spain by Rieusset and Eurobinder.
ALL RIGHTS RESERVED

ISBN 0 671 07616 7

Acknowledgement
The publishers would like to thank the staff of
Art for Eating for their assistance.

CAKES &
CAKE DECORATION

Exeter Books

NEW YORK

Contents

11in round
10in square

5¼ hours

275°F

1⅓ cups

7

3½ cups

1½ cups

1½ tblsp

7 tblsp

1¾ tsp

2 lemons

2 oranges

¾ tsp

1½ cups

3⅓ cups

1¾ cups

2¾ cups

5oz

5oz

2¼ tblsp

3¼ tblsp

Introduction

Cake decorating is both rewarding and interesting. It is hoped that this book will show how simple it can be and encourage those who use it to improve on their basic skills.

Starting with the simplest frostings, such as butter frosting, which is easy to use and can create elaborate novelty cakes, the book gradually introduces the more complex techniques required to master the frosting and decoration of wedding and other celebration cakes.

Always try to avoid last-minute rushes; many of the decorations can be made in advance and stored. Try to plan ahead when you know that you will be making a special cake and remember that frosting and decorating can take time and patience. If you have not had much

practice, start with the simpler designs before trying to tackle a royal-frosted celebration cake. You will be anxious that the result should be stunning, so practice first!

Never push the frosting design straight onto the cake, as you may ruin the surface you have created. If you are using a complex design, apply it first in white frosting then go over it in color. This way, if you make a mistake, you will not have not stained the surface of the cake. The cakes in this book will certainly give you some new ideas and may encourage you to design versions of your own.

Cakes and their decoration is an absorbing hobby. By following and practising some of the designs suggested, it is hoped you will be able to produce a highly professional result – cakes for every occasion.

Note:
All eggs are size 2.
All spoon measures are level.
Cooking times may vary as they depend upon the efficiency of your oven. Dishes should always be placed in the center of the oven unless otherwise stated.
Fan-assisted ovens may cook slightly quicker, so follow the manufacturer's instructions.
Always preheat the oven to the specified temperature.

Marzipan or Almond Paste

This is a paste which is made firm and rollable, and is traditionally used as a base cover for fruit cakes before coating with royal frosting or any other decorative frosting. Prepare the cake by levelling the top, if necessary. Dust a work surface with confectioners' sugar and roll out half the almond paste 1 inch larger than the top of the cake. Brush the top of the cake with the apricot glaze, or the egg white and brandy. Invert the cake onto the almond paste and, using a palette knife, draw up the top of the almond paste around the cake. Put the top of the cake down on a board and brush the sides of the cake with apricot glaze. Cut two pieces of string or thread, one the height of the cake and the other equal in length to the circumference. Roll out the remaining almond paste into a strip, equal in width and length to the circumference of the cake, using the strings as a guide, or cut two short strips of paste instead. Carefully wrap the almond paste round the cake, pressing firmly round the sides and joins. For a square cake, cut the string into four lengths, equal to the sides of the cake and cut the paste to match. Press lightly on the paste when it is placed round the cake in order to produce sharp corners. When covered, leave the cake for 24 hours to dry. Wedding cakes should be left for up to 1 week before frosting, otherwise almond oil will stain the frosting if the cake is kept after the wedding.

Marzipan or Almond Paste

PREPARATION TIME: 15 minutes

½ cup sugar
½ cup confectioners' sugar
1 cup ground almonds
1 tsp lemon juice
A few drops almond essence
1 or 2 egg yolks, beaten

Mix the sugars and the ground almonds in a bowl. Make a well in the center and add the lemon juice, almond essence and egg yolk or yolks to the mixture and form into a pliable dough. Lightly dust the work surface with confectioners'

Guide to Almond Paste Quantities Required for Cakes

Square	Round	Almond Paste/Marzipan
5 inch	6 inch	12oz
6 inch	7 inch	1lb 4oz
7 inch	8 inch	1½lb
8 inch	9 inch	1½lb
9 inch	10 inch	2lb
10 inch	11 inch	2¼lb
11 inch	12 inch	2½lb
12 inch		3lb

sugar and turn out the dough. Knead until smooth. The almond paste can be stored in a polythene bag or wrapped in foil for 2-3 days before use. Makes 1lb.

Apricot Glaze

PREPARATION TIME: 10 minutes

This glaze can be stored in an airtight container for up to 1 week, if kept in the refrigerator. Re-boil the glaze and cool before applying to the cake.

6-8oz apricot jam
2 tblsp water

Put the jam and water in a saucepan and heat until the jam has melted, stirring occasionally. Pour the jam through a sieve and return it to a clean saucepan. Re-boil and simmer until you have a slightly thickened consistency. Cool before applying to the cake.

How to Royal Frost

It does not matter whether you frost the top or the sides first, the important point to remember is that the frosting should be applied in several thin coats. Try frosting a section first, rather than doing all of it in one go. Your aim is to achieve a smooth surface and you must let each coat dry before applying another. Most cakes require 2 coats on the top and sides, with maybe 3 on the top for a very smooth finish. Wedding cakes require three coats all over and the bottom tiers need 4 coats. For a 2 or 3-tier cake apply 4 coats to the bottom tier; for a 4-tier cake apply 4 coats to the bottom 2 tiers.

Method for Frosting a Cake – Frosting the Sides of a Round Cake

A flat-sided scraper is essential for producing smooth sides. Put plenty of frosting on the side of the cake and, using a small palette knife, move it back and forth to get a relatively smooth surface and to remove little air pockets. For round cakes, put your arm round the back of the cake and move the scraper forwards on the cake as this will help you to get a smooth, sweeping movement without stopping. The scraper should be upright against the side of the cake. Move the scraper off the cake at an angle so the join is not noticeable. If you use a turntable, it will make frosting larger cakes easier. Hold the scraper to the side of the cake and use the other hand round the cake so the turntable moves round quickly and smoothly in one revolution. Scrape off any extra frosting with a small palette knife. Wipe the cake board and allow each coat to dry for 2-3 hours or overnight before frosting the top.

Frosting the Top

When frosting the base tier of a wedding cake, remember not to add glycerine. Spread the frosting on the cake and, using a metal, or firm plastic, ruler held at a 30° angle, draw it gently across the cake with a positive movement. Try not to press down too hard or the frosting will be too thin. Remove any surplus frosting from the sides of the cake with a clean palette knife. Leave the frosting to dry for at least a day. Remove any rough edges round the joins with clean, fine-graded sandpaper. If the coating is not enough, repeat this 2-3 times. Wait 24 hours before applying frosting decoration onto the cake.

Frosting a Square Cake

Ice 2 opposite sides first, then the other 2 sides to produce sharp corners. Hold the palette knife parallel with the side of the cake when frosting.

Royal Frosting

The consistency of royal frosting depends upon its use. For rosettes and flat frosting it should be quite firm, whereas for applying latticework and writing it should be a little thinner. When frosting is required for any flooding and runouts, it should be thin and smooth. Royal frosting can be made in any quantity in the proportion of 1 egg per cup of sieved confectioners' sugar. Keep the frosting bowl covered with a damp cloth to keep it moist. As an egg substitute, egg albumen (white) can be bought in specialist cake decoration shops and the instructions for use are given on the packet. The addition of glycerine will aid the softening of the frosting when it is dry. This makes it easier to cut.

Wedding Cakes

When frosting wedding cakes, do not add glycerine to the two top layers of frosting on the bottom tier, so the cake can support the other tiers. Made frosting can be stored in an airtight container in a cool atmosphere for 2 days. Before use the stored frosting should be stirred well.

Beat the egg whites with a wire whisk until frothy, making sure that the bowl is clean and dry first. Gradually beat in half the confectioners' sugar using a wooden spoon. Beat in the remaining half of the confectioners' sugar with the glycerine and, if using lemon juice, add it now. Beat the mixture thoroughly until smooth and white. Beat in enough icing sugar to give the mixture a consistency which is stiff and stands in peaks. Add the color, if required. Cover the bowl with a damp cloth and leave the frosting to stand for several hours. This allows any air bubbles to rise to the surface of the frosting and burst. Before using, stir well with a wooden spoon. Do not overbeat. Note: if you are using an electric mixer, use the slowest speed and leave the frosting for 24 hours as this will incorporate more air and will need longer to stand.

Facing page: covering with almond paste, and using apricot glaze.

Lining
All pan
unless
cake pa
manufa
If using
base ne
sponge
mixtur
If you a
which
the sid
lining u
wax pa

Chocolate
Blend 2 tblsp cocoa powder with 2 tblsp boiling water. Cool, then add to the mixture with 1 tblsp milk.

Coffee
Replace 1 tblsp milk with 1 tblsp coffee essence.

Crème au Beurre

PREPARATION TIME: 15 minutes

2 egg whites
½ cup confectioners' sugar, sifted
½ cup unsalted butter
Flavorings (see 'Variations')

Place the egg whites and confectioners' sugar in a bowl over a pan of simmering water. Beat until the mixture holds its shape. Cool. Cream the butter until soft then beat into the egg white mixture, a little at a time. Flavor or color as required.

Variations

Chocolate
Melt 2oz plain chocolate in a bowl over a pan of hot water. Cool and beat into the egg white mixture.

Coffee
Add 1 tblsp coffee essence to the egg white mixture.

Praline
Gently heat ¼ cup of both sugar and blanched almonds in a small pan until the sugar turns brown round the nuts. Turn the mixture onto an oiled cooky sheet, cool and crush with a rolling pin. Add the 3 tblsp of this crushed praline to the egg white mixture.
NB: this frosting can be stored in an airtight container in the

Guide to Royal Frosting Quantities Requir to Flat Frost in Two Thin Coats

Square	Round	Icing Sugar
5 inch	6 inch	1½lb
6 inch	7 inch	2lb
7 inch	8 inch	2½lb
8 inch	9 inch	3lb
9 inch	10 inch	3½lb
10 inch	11 inch	3½lb
11 inch	12 inch	4½lb
12 inch		4½lb

Molding Frosting

PREPARATION TIME: 20 minutes

This is also known as kneaded fondant. It is very easy to use and can be rolled out like pastry. It is ideal for covering novelty cakes and even rich fruit cake. The frosting sets and becomes firm. Molding frosting can be used to cover a cake directly or over almond paste. If using almond paste first, allow the paste to dry before covering with the frosting, which can also be used to make flowers and other decorations.

2 cups confectioners' sugar
1 egg white
¼ cup liquid glucose
Food coloring or flavoring, if desired

Sift the confectioners' sugar into a mixing bowl and add the egg white and the liquid glucose to the center of the sugar. Beat the ingredients with a wooden spoon, gradually incorporating the confectioners' sugar to result in a stiff mixture. Knead the frosting until you have a pliable paste. This icing can be stored by placing it into a bag, wrapping it in plastic wrap or sealing it in a plastic container and storing it in a cool place for up to 3 days. If adding a color, sprinkle with a little more sifted confectioners' sugar to keep the frosting the same consistency.

To Apply Molding or Gelatin Frosting

Brush either the cake with apricot glaze or the almond paste with egg white. Roll out the frosting on a surface dusted with confectioners' sugar or cornstarch, or between two sheets of dusted polythene. Roll out the frosting at least 3 inches larger than the top of the

cake. Support the frosting on a rolling pin and drape it over th cake. Dust your hands with cornstarch or confectioners' su and rub the surface of the cake working in circular movements with the palms of your hands t make the frosting thinner and it down the sides of the cake. Smooth out any folds in the frosting and cut off the excess. frosting a square cake, mold th corners so that the square keep shape. Leave to dry.

Gelatin Frosting

PREPARATION TIME: 20 minu

This frosting can be used in the same way as molding frosting, b when it dries it becomes quite brittle. The frosting can be used make decorations such as flowe and leaves.

2 tsp gelatin powder
2 tblsp water to dissolve the gelati
2 cups confectioners' sugar
1 egg white

Put the gelatin powder into the water, which is contained in a small, heatproof basin held over saucepan of hot water. Stir until the gelatin has dissolved. Sift the confectioners' sugar into another bowl and add the dissolved gelat and egg white. Stir well until firm then knead with the fingers until smooth. Dust with extra confectioners' sugar, if necessary. adding food coloring, sprinkle wit more confectioners' sugar to keep the frosting to the same consistency. This frosting can be stored for 2 to 3 days before use. To do so, wrap it in plastic wrap o

Novelty Cakes

the top of the cake). Fit a pastry bag with a small star tip and fill with royal frosting. Pipe shells round the bottom edge of the cake. Put the lid on a basin and apply frosted shells round the edge of the lid. Decorate the lid with either fresh or piped flowers and a bow secured with royal frosting. Place the candies on top of the cake and put the lid on, leaving them partially revealed.

Clown

1lb molding frosting
6 tblsp colored pale orange
¾ cup colored yellow
⅔ cup colored red
¼ cup colored green
1 large jelly roll
4 small jelly rolls
2 Lady fingers (sponge fingers)
1 marshmallow
1 recipe apricot glaze
1 recipe royal frosting, colored red

Using the orange molding frosting, break off 2 small rounds and gently flatten them. Make 4 cuts halfway into the balls to make fingers. Roll out the remaining orange frosting into a strip which is 8x3 inches. Brush the ends of the jelly roll with the apricot glaze and use the orange strip to cover the ends of the jelly roll. Brush the rest of the jelly roll with the glaze and with a third of the yellow frosting rolled out into a strip 8x5 inches, cover the glazed area of jelly roll. Squeeze the join of the yellow and orange frosting so that it forms a head and body. Stand the jelly roll upright on a cake board with something for support. Put the small jelly rolls lengthways for the legs and brush with glaze. Take a small ball of yellow molding frosting and roll it out into a 4x1 inch width. Divide it into 2 and cut slashes in each

These are fun cakes enjoyed by all ages, but particularly by children. There follows a variety of designs which can be used for every occasion. It is suggested that you use the quick cake mixture or maderia cake for these. Hopefully, this will inspire you to design your own novelty cakes which might be more appropriate for a specific occasion. If you find it difficult to find a cake board for an unusual cake, make your own by covering a sheet of thick card with silver foil.

Birthday Box

12x10x2 inch quick mix cake
Recipe apricot glaze
8oz almond paste (optional) – this
   makes the cake a little smoother
Recipe molding frosting
Thin 12x10 inch cake board or piece
   of thick card
Food coloring – yellow
8oz candies
8oz royal frosting
Egg white, beaten, for attaching
   molding frosting

Put the cake on a larger cake board. Brush with apricot glaze and cover, if desired, with a thin layer of almond paste. Color the molding frosting and save 4oz in a plastic bag. Brush the cake with egg white, roll out the molding frosting and use it to cover the almond pasted cake. With a knife or ruler press lines diagonally into the frosting. Roll out the reserved 4oz of molding frosting and cover the white side of a thin, rectangular, silver cake board (the same size as

This page: Birthday Box.

Facing page: Clown.

halfway up. These will be used for the hair (reserve). Brush the sponge fingers with glaze and cover them with yellow fondant. Stick them with jam onto the sides of the body. Roll out the remaining yellow frosting into a strip 8x5 inches and cut it down the middle. Use each strip to cover the legs. Roll out a small piece of red frosting and mold it over the marshmallow and leave to dry. Roll out 2 pea-sized balls of red frosting and use them as buttons. Roll out another small piece of red frosting and cut with a pastry cutter. Divide the green frosting into two balls, rolling out one and cutting with the same round pastry cutter. Using a cocktail stick, create folds in the circles which radiate from the center. Work your way round. Cut one of the circles in two and the other into four. Roll out the red frosting into an oblong 7x3 inches and attach it to the legs in thin strips. Using the reserved green frosting, flatten it a little and cut it into two, shaping each half into an oval. Stick them upright on to the end of the legs as boots. Put half red and half green frills round the neck of the clown, securing them with a little apricot glaze. Put quarter frills round his wrists and ankles, with a little glaze to attach them to the hands. Secure the hair

to his head with glaze. Do the same with the hat. Fill a pastry bag fitted with a writing tip with the red frosting and pipe features onto the clown's face. Surround him with sweets or put balloons in his hand.

Giant Sandwich Cake

12x10x2 inch quick mix cake
Food colorings – brown, green, yellow, pink, red
Recipe molding frosting
Egg white to brush almond paste
½ x recipe butter cream frosting
8oz almond paste, if required

Cut the cake diagonally so you have 2 triangles. Color half of the frosting pale brown. Divide a further quarter into four and color the pieces green, yellow, salmon pink and red. Remember to keep frosting in a plastic bag when you are not using it, to prevent it from drying out. For the lettuce, roll out an irregular shape with the green frosting and crinkle it up using a cocktail stick so it looks like ruched material. Reserve on a sheet of non-stick silicone paper. To make the ham, roll out the pink frosting with a pinch of white frosting, making sure the colors stay separate. Roll out into an oval shape and reserve. For the cheese, roll the yellow frosting into a 4 inch square and reserve. For the tomato slices, roll the red frosting into a 4 inch square and with a small, plain round pastry cutter cut rounds. Roll out the pale brown frosting into 6 strips all 2 inches wide: two

12 inches long, two 10 inches long, two 16 inches long. Use the egg white to brush the sides of the triangles. Stick the brown strips onto the appropriate length sides. Roll out the remaining white frosting into a triangle large enough to cover the top of one triangular cake piece. Brush the top of the cake triangle and fix on the molding frosting triangle. Spread the top of the other cake, the one without white molding frosting, with a little butter frosting to make the bottom half of the sandwich and make sure it is on either a presentation plate or a cake board. Around the edges of the bottom triangle lay the lettuce, ham, tomato and cheese so they spill out of the cake. Stick together with the frosted triangle. Fit a pastry bag with a star tip and fill with the remaining butter frosting. Frost irregular swirls in between the lettuce, tomato, cheese and ham. Dust the top of the triangular cake with a little confectioners' sugar.

Birthday Breakfast

Rich fruit cake (measure the size of your skillet and bake a cake that will fit)
Recipe apricot glaze
4oz white molding frosting
Food colorings – brown, pink
15oz can apricot halves

Transfer the fruit cake to the frying pan. Brush the top with apricot glaze. Roll out the white molding frosting and cut into several irregular shapes, rounding off any sharp corners. Roll the remaining frosting into sausage shapes and brush them with a little brown and pink food coloring. Drain the can of apricot halves. Place the irregular white molding frosting shapes on top of the cake, putting an inverted apricot half on each one. Put the sausages in the pan. Brush the sausages and the apricot halves with a little apricot glaze.

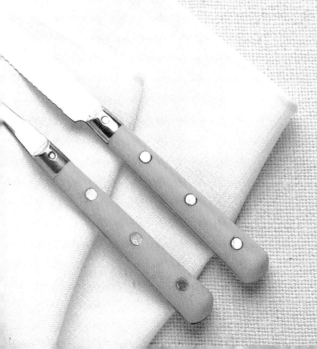

Giant Sandwich Cake (top left) and Birthday Breakfast (bottom left).

Camelot Castle

2 8 inch square 6-egg Victoria sponges
Recipe butter cream frosting
Recipe apricot glaze
4 ice cream cones
4 miniature jelly rolls
1 rectangular plain cooky
1 water cooky
½ cup granulated sugar
4oz molding frosting
Recipe royal frosting
Sugar flowers
Silver balls
3 or 4 small paper flags
Food colorings – pink, green, red

Toffee Water (To Fill Moat)
1 cup granulated sugar
⅔ cup water
Blue food coloring
Sugar thermometer, if available

Cut a 2 inch wide slice from one cake. Put the other cake towards the back of the cake board. Stick the large section of cake to the cake on the board with some butter frosting. Make sure it sits towards the back of the base cake. With apricot glaze, secure the 2 inch slice on the front edge of the cake board. Using apricot glaze, brush the ends of the small jelly rolls and place them in the four corners of the cake, placing the ice cream cones on top. Cover the small jelly rolls, ice cream cones and the top and sides of the cake with butter frosting. Also frost the 2 inch slice. Put the water cooky on the front side of the cake between the 2 jelly roll towers. Put the granulated sugar, with a few drops of pink food coloring, in a bowl and stir well until the sugar takes up the color. Sprinkle the colored sugar over the ice-cream cones, the top of the castle and the grounds. Fit a star tip to a pastry bag and fill with royal frosting. Pipe round the top of the castle walls and over the front surface of the water cooky. When the stars are just drying, go round the top of the walls and frost another row of stars on top of each alternate star. Put a silver ball in the center of each of the stars round the edge of the door and 2 for doorknobs. Color a little of the royal frosting green, and a little red, and frost the green vine with red stars for flowers. You can also use sugar flowers.

To Make the Water to Fill the Moat
Color the molding frosting green and roll it out to form a long sausage which will go round the edge of the board. Use the frosting

with a pastry wheel. With a little water, attach the ribbons of fondant to the inside of the shoes approximately halfway between the toe and heel. With a cocktail stick, gently mark round the top of the shoe, then the sole. Cut two 6 inch long, string-width strips of fondant and make a little bow out of each and put them in place. As an alternative, pink satin ribbon can be used in place of fondant. Fill the shoes with the candies.

Football Boot

10x8 inch quick mix cake
Jam for filling
Recipe apricot glaze
Recipe molding frosting
Recipe butter frosting
¼ cup shredded coconut
¼ cup chocolate chips
Food coloring – red, yellow, black and
  green
Medium star tip and pastry bag
2 liquorice laces
12 inch square cake board
1 cocktail stick

Cut the cake horizontally and stick together with jam for filling. Put the cakes on the board. With a cocktail stick mark out the outline of the boot. When you are happy with the outline, cut it out with a sharp knife and brush with apricot glaze. Divide the molding frosting into two, remembering to keep the frosting in a plastic bag when not in use. Roll out half the frosting into an oblong and cover the boot shape (top and sides). Do not frost the leg. Cut the frosting at the ankle to indicate the top of the boot. Divide the remaining frosting into two, coloring half red and the rest yellow. Draw out the shapes for the patches, tongue of the boot and the flash on some wax paper. Draw a large 'E' with a double line and cut it out. This should be used as a template to guide you when you roll out the red frosting to cover the ankle and the flash for the side of the boot. Roll out the yellow molding frosting and cut the

to form a wall and stick it down by smoothing it onto the board, then leave it to dry for one hour. Heat the sugar and water so the sugar dissolves and boils. Continue to boil the mixture until it reaches 'soft crack' point, that is, just before it starts to color. If a sugar thermometer is available, the reading should be 270-290°F. Pour the sugar mixture into the moat. Put the sugar flowers on the green banks of the moat and lay the cooky across from the castle to the land to form a drawbridge. Use the flags to decorate.

Ballet Shoes

2 jelly rolls
12 inch square cake board
2lb fondant frosting
Food coloring – pink
Recipe apricot glaze
Cornstarch to dust
4 tblsp jam
1 yard pink satin ribbon (as an
  alternative to fondant ribbons)

To Make Shoes
Cut the edge of one end of the cake into a point. Then cut the tip of the point. This will be the toe end of the shoe. Repeat for the other shoe and place them both on

the cake board. Cut the other end of the cake, rounding it slightly. Cut out a long oval towards the heel end of the cake. Press the cake in firmly, but gently, to create an instep. Color all the fondant pale pink. Brush the cake with the glaze. Roll out the fondant on the cornstarch-dusted work surface. Press the fondant down and smooth out any cracks. Mold it gently round the toe and take special care to squeeze and tuck it into the inside of the shoe. Cut off any excess and re-mold it into a ball. Roll out. Cut 4 long strips 1 inch wide and cut the shortest ends with pinking shears or cut

This page: Camelot Castle.

Facing page: Ballet Shoes (top) and Football Boot (bottom).

same shapes, but smaller, to go on top of the red. Cut the liquorice laces and tie into a bow. With a little frosting place it at the ankle. Mix half of the butter frosting yellow and half red. Fill a pastry bag with the red butter frosting and pipe a band about 6 stripes wide, then repeat with the yellow frosting. Work your way up the leg until you have 3 red bands and 2 yellow. Put rows of chocolate chips on the side of the boot to represent studs. Put the shredded coconut in a bowl and add a few drops of green food color. Stir in and use to sprinkle on the board to represent grass.

Shirt and Tie

15x3½x¾ inch quick mix cake
2 x recipe butter cream frosting
4oz colored fondant, if using design with tie
1 small packet round candies, e.g. jellies
Food coloring – red

In a clean bowl reserve ¼ of the butter cream frosting and with the food coloring make up a darker shade of the color previously used. Wash the pan used for baking the cake and, if the pan is old or marked, line with foil so that it is totally covered both inside and out. Alternatively, you could make or use a cardboard shirt box. Put the cake into the cake pan or box, and spread with the lighter frosting. If the cake fits snugly into its box or pan, only frost the top; if not, frost all the visible cake. Make the neck and collar shaping by first marking it out. Draw a line in the frosting with a cocktail stick 3 inches from one end of the cake. (The 9 inch sides are top and bottom.) This marks the shoulder line, so use this line to guide you when building up the collar with more frosting. Half the collar (front and back) should be on either side of the faint line. Fill the pastry bag with the darker frosting and with a writing tip outline the collar and shoulder seam. Roll out a thin strip of fondant 1½ inches wide and 14 inches long, pinch it in to form the tie knot and place on the cake. If you are using the design with center placket (shirt front) pocket and sleeves use the darker frosting in the pastry bag and frost the shirt front, pocket and sleeves. Put the candies in position as buttons.

Artist's Palette

9 inch square quick mix cake
Recipe apricot glaze
¾lb molding frosting
½ cup granulated sugar
Food colorings – red, blue, green, yellow, orange, violet and brown

Cut a kidney shape out of the cake and carefully cut a circle slightly off center. Place the cake on the cake board and brush with apricot glaze. Color all except 2oz of the molding frosting pale brown. Roll out and use to cover the palette, pushing in gently at the hole so that the frosting coats the inner wall of the circle. Push down to reveal the cake board. Using a dry brush, dip gently into the brown food coloring and drag hesitantly across the palette. Wipe the brush with kitchen paper to absorb some of the food coloring and continue to cover the palette with the wood grain. Leave to dry. Color 1 tblsp of granulated sugar with each of the food colorings. This is done by adding a few drops and stirring until the sugar absorbs the color. Roll out the remaining molding frosting into a long sausage shape and cut in half. Make a point at the end of one sausage and leave to dry and gently flatten the end of the other.

To Make the Pencil and Paintbrush
When the molding frosting shapes are dry, copying a pencil, color the one with the pointed end by painting in the lead and the outside. Copy the brush you are using and place them next to the palette. When the palette is dry, put little mounds of the colored sugar on the top.

Pugwash at Sea

11½x8½x1½ inch quick mix cake
Recipe royal frosting
Recipe butter frosting
8oz molding frosting
Recipe apricot glaze
1 packet of mints with a hole
1 black liquorice candy
1 tiny paper flag on a cocktail stick
Food colorings – including blue

Cut a 4 inch slice from the shortest side of the cake. From the smallest cake cut 2 inch slice from one end. Cut a point out of the remaining rectangle measuring 6½x4 inches.

Artist's Palette (left) and Shirt
and Tie (below).

Coconut mushrooms, if available
¼ cup shredded coconut
Candle and holder

Put the cakes on top of one another. Cut them in an irregular 'T' shape with a round top. Use the butter cream to layer the cakes together. Stand the cakes up so they resemble a 'T' shape on a 9 inch heart-shaped cake board. Brush the layered cakes with the apricot glaze. Roll out the almond paste and cover the cake with a thin layer. Divide the molding frosting into two and color half red. Roll out the red molding frosting, reserving 2oz to cover the top bar of the 'T', and use egg white to brush the almond paste so the frosting will adhere. Roll out the white frosting, reserving 4oz, and use it to cover the non-frosted section of the cake. Roll out the reserved 4oz of white molding frosting and cut small circles. Dot them on the red roof. Roll out the 2oz of the red molding frosting and cut 2 circles, 1 inch in diameter, for windows and a rectangle for a door. Color a little royal frosting green and decorate with leaves on the side of the house. Make frosted curtains on the windows and the arch round the door. Use the sugar flowers to decorate the house and garden. Put the shredded coconut in a bowl with a few drops of green coloring, mix well and use the coconut to decorate the board like grass. Stand the coconut mushrooms on the grass and put the candle holder with candle on the roof to represent the chimney.

Place the remaining 8½x7 inch cake on a cake board. Stick the pointed cake to the top of the large cake then stick the 2 inch strip on top of that to form a cabin. Brush the two pieces of cake with apricot glaze. Color the molding frosting with your favorite color and roll it out to cover the ship. Using a pastry bag fitted with a writing tip and filled with royal frosting, write the name of the ship and pipe on the doors and windows. Use a little frosting to secure the liquorice candy on top of the cabin as a funnel. Cotton wool may be used to simulate smoke. Color the butter frosting with a little blue food coloring and spoon it over the large cake to form waves. Use a fork to peak the frosting, but do not overmix or the frosting will go green! Put the flag at the front of the boat and with a little frosting, stick the mints onto the deck to represent life belts.

Radio

8 inch round quick mix cake
Recipe apricot glaze
Recipes gelatin or molding frosting
6oz jam
Food coloring – brown, pink, black,
  non-toxic gold
1 egg white, beaten
Recipe royal frosting

Cut a crescent off one side of the cake so it will stand up on its side. Place the cake on a 9-inch square cake board. Brush the cake all over with apricot glaze. Tint the frosting pink and roll it out. Cover the cake completely and leave to dry. Take the remaining frosting, re-mold it and tint it a little darker. Roll it out into a rectangle and cut into 6 strips to make the starburst. Cut two circles for the knobs and a semi-circle for the dial. Stick all the decoration on the cake with egg white. Fill a pastry bag with royal frosting and fit it with a writing tip. Frost the mesh by decorating

diagonally between the starburst. Decorate on the lines for the dial, tuner knob and 'on/off' switch. Finally, pipe a decorative triangle on the board under each knob, with another smaller triangle over the top. Leave the frosting to dry. Using a small paintbrush, paint the mesh and trim with non-toxic gold food coloring and the inside of the mesh with diagonal lines of black food coloring.

House on the Hill

2 11½x8½x1½ inch quick mix cakes
2 recipe apricot glaze
1½ recipe molding frosting
Food colorings – red, green
Recipe butter frosting
Recipe royal frosting
16oz almond paste
Sugar flowers

Snowman

1¾ pint) pudding basin quick mix
  cake
⅔ pint pudding basin quick mix
  cake; use a 2½ pint mixture
  altogether
Recipe American frosting
A few round candies or liquorice
  candies for buttons and features
8 inch length of ribbon
Paper hat, optional

When the cakes have cooled on a wire rack, trim the smaller cake

This page: Radio Cake. Facing page: House on the Hill (top) and Pugwash at Sea (bottom).

round the wider edge to round it off. Spread the jam on the top of the larger cake and sit the smaller on top of the larger cake to form the head and body on the cake board. Cover the cakes completely with the American frosting. Select the candies or liquorice assortment candies for features and buttons. Decorate with a hat and a ribbon scarf.

Kitchen

8 inch square Madeira cake
Recipe royal frosting
Recipe apricot glaze
1lb molding frosting
Food colorings – red, green, orange, silver

Toffee Water
1 cup granulated sugar
⅔ cup water
Sugar thermometer, if available

Cut the cake in half and form an 'L' shape on a 12 inch cake board. Halfway along one piece of cake, cut a 1 inch square hole. Roll out half the molding frosting, brush the cake with apricot glaze and use the frosting to cover the 'L' shape. Color three-quarters of the remaining frosting red and use half rolled out and laid on the inside of the rectangle of the 'L'. Using a knife, mark ½ inch squares and press down gently. Do not cut through the frosting. Roll out the remaining red frosting and cut into small squares to form tiles for the work surface. Spread the rectangle of cake without the hole cut into it with a little royal frosting and stick down the small squares with a little frosting surrounding each. Cut two 2 inch squares and use one to line the hole, gently pushing in the corners. Place the other square alongside as a draining board. Use a knife to indent the board.

To Make Faucets
Take a pinch from the remaining white frosting and roll out into a small sausage shape. Cut in half, and with a small pair of scissors snip lengthways down the end once and again crossing the cut. Splay out the 4 pieces. Curl the other end of the sausage to form the waterspout. Repeat with the other small sausage shape and leave them both to dry.

To Make the Vegetables
Take a pinch from the remaining

white molding frosting. Color it green and shape about two-thirds into a small ball for the heart of the cabbage. Shape the remainder into 8 leaves and arrange the leaves around the heart, overlapping each one. Press gently so that they adhere to one another. Taking another pinch from the white, color it orange and shape into small cones. Make a little piece green and cut out some stalks. Press them to the tops of the carrot. To make the peas, shape any small pieces of green molding frosting into balls. Color a small pinch of molding frosting red and form into small balls. Make more green stalks and, with a cocktail stick, dent the top of each ball and push in a little green stalk to make tomatoes.

To Make Plates
Roll out any odd pieces of colored molding frosting into tiny balls. Mold a few round the end of a pencil and flatten some gently. Reserve them until you have made the sugar water. Color a little royal frosting red and use to fill a pastry bag fitted with a writing tip. Frost the knobs and drawers on the inside of the kitchen. Using a small paintbrush, paint the faucets with silver non-toxic coloring. Leave them to dry.

To Make the Sugar Water
Heat the sugar and water so that the sugar dissolves and boils. Continue to boil the mixture until it reaches a soft crack point – that

is, just before it starts to color. If a sugar thermometer is available, the reading should be 270-290°F. Pour the sugar mixture into the sink and push in the plates and dishes before it sets. Using a little royal frosting, put the faucets into place.

The Mouse that got the Cheese

8 inch square Madeira sponge
2 x recipe butter frosting
2 eyes, as used in dollmaking
1 yard pink cord
2 inch diameter teardrop shapes of pink paper
1 jelly candy
2 cocktail sticks
Food coloring – black

Mouse
Cut the cake diagonally and stand it upright on the diagonal line. Round the top of the triangle to give the mouse a smooth back. With a little black food coloring, color half the butter frosting so it is light grey. Cover all the exposed areas of the cake and peak it gently with a fork. Cut 12 inches of pink cord and attach it to one end for a tail. Cut 6 inch lengths and knot them all in the middle. Push them onto the front of his face, placing the jelly sweet on the knot. Attach the tear drop shapes to the side of his head for ears using the cocktail sticks. Place an eye on each side of his head.

Cheese
Put the remaining triangle on one end and, with a melon baller, scoop out little holes. Cover the cake with the remaining butter frosting and smooth gently with a palette knife.

Christmas Pudding

This makes a quick, non-frosted Christmas cake which acts as a centerpiece for a party, or for a family Christmas.

9 inch recipe for rich fruit cake baked in a 1¾ pint ovenproof pudding basin
6 tblsp brandy
8oz almond paste
Recipe apricot glaze
½ recipe royal frosting
Holly to decorate

After cooking, soak the fruit cake with the brandy. As the cake is not frosted this will keep it moist. Put the cake on a cake board or plate. Roll out the almond paste into a circle and push it into an irregular shape, like a little island with coves. Brush the top and a little way down the cake with the apricot glaze. Cover the top and the sides of the cake with the almond paste. Fit a pastry bag with a large star tip and fill with royal frosting. Decorate with large frosted stars round the base of the cake. Decorate with real almond paste or artificial holly.

This page: Kitchen (top) and The Mouse that got the Cheese (bottom).

Facing page: Snowman and Christmas Pudding Cake.

Tea Time Treats

Baking at home is not as difficult as some might expect and in very little time one can create some appetizing treats for the tea table. Here are lots of recipes which may tempt you to try them for yourself at picnics, birthdays and tea parties.

Biscuits

PREPARATION TIME: 15 minutes
COOKING TIME: 10-15 minutes
OVEN TEMPERATURE: 400°F

2 cups all-purpose flour
1 tsp cream of tartar
½ tsp bicarbonate of soda
Good pinch of salt
3 tblsp butter or margarine
6 tblsp superfine sugar
3 tblsp white raisins
1 tblsp sugared ginger pieces
1 tblsp sunflower seeds
2 eggs, plus a little milk if required
1 egg, beaten or a little milk for glazing

Sieve the dry ingredients twice. Cut in the fat, add sugar, white raisins, ginger pieces and sunflower seeds and mix to a soft dough with eggs. Knead lightly on floured surface. Roll out to approximately ½ inch thickness. Place on floured cooky sheet and brush the top with beaten egg or milk. Bake in the oven for 10-15 minutes.

Walnut Cake

PREPARATION TIME: 15 minutes
COOKING TIME: 35 minutes
OVEN TEMPERATURE: 350°F

4 eggs
¾ cup superfine sugar
1 cup all-purpose flour, sifted
1 tblsp oil
½ cup walnuts, finely chopped
Recipe butter cream
Walnut halves to decorate

Grease and line two 8 inch cake pans. Place the eggs and sugar in a heatproof bowl and beat over a pan of hot, but not boiling, water until thick (see beaten sponge method). Partially fold in the flour, add the oil and chopped walnuts and fold in gently. Divide the mixture between the prepared pans and bake in the oven for 35 minutes. When the cake is cooked it will spring back when touched. Turn onto a wire rack to cool. Split each cake in half and fill with butter cream. Swirl the remaining butter cream on top of the cake and decorate with walnut halves.

Welsh Cakes (above), Walnut Cake (right) and Biscuits (far right).

Welsh Cakes

PREPARATION TIME: 15 minutes
COOKING TIME: 8 minutes (4 minutes per side)
OVEN TEMPERATURE: 275°F

1 cup all-purpose flour
1 tsp baking powder
3 tblsp sugar
3 tblsp butter or margarine
½ tsp ground nutmeg
3 tblsp currants
1 egg, plus a little milk if required
Pinch of salt

Sieve the flour, baking powder and salt. Cut in the fat and stir in sugar, nutmeg and currants. Mix to a pastry consistency with egg. Roll out to ¼ inch thickness and cut with a ¼ inch small biscuit cutter. Cook on baking stone or large greased pan. Switch oven off for 15 minutes then grease and reheat for second batch. Dredge with superfine sugar and serve. Makes 10.

Flapjacks

PREPARATION TIME: 15 minutes

COOKING TIME: 30 minutes

OVEN TEMPERATURE: 350°F

½ cup margarine
½ cup soft brown sugar
6 tblsp corn syrup
1 cup rolled oats

Melt the margarine, sugar and syrup in a bowl over a pan of hot water. Stir in the rolled oats and mix thoroughly. Grease a shallow 8 inch square pan. Turn the mixture into the pan and smooth down the top. Bake in the oven for 30 minutes until golden. Cool in the pan for 3 minutes before cutting into fingers. Remove from pan when cool. Makes 16.

Coconut Specials

PREPARATION TIME: 20 minutes

COOKING TIME: 30 minutes

OVEN TEMPERATURE: 325°F

8oz puff pastry
A little jam, melted
4 tblsp melted butter
½ cup shredded coconut
½ cup sugar
2 eggs

Roll out the puff pastry. Using a round cooky cutter, cut rounds and use to line a patty pan. Using a pastry brush, coat the pastry with a little jam. Beat together the butter, coconut, sugar and eggs. Divide the coconut mixture between the patty pans. Bake in the oven for 30 minutes until golden brown. When cooked, remove from pan and cool on a wire rack. Makes 14.

Victoria Sponge

PREPARATION TIME: 30 minutes

COOKING TIME: 20-25 minutes

OVEN TEMPERATURE: 375°F

A stick of butter or margarine
½ cup sugar
2 eggs
1 cup cake flour, sifted with a pinch of
  salt
1¼ tsp baking powder
1 tblsp hot water

3 tblsp jam
⅔ cup heavy cream, whipped
Confectioners' sugar

Grease and line two 7 inch cake pans. Cream the fat and sugar until light and fluffy. Beat in the eggs singly and fold in 1 tblsp of flour with each egg. Fold in the remaining flour, then add the hot water. Divide the mixture between the pans and bake in the oven for 20-25 minutes until the cakes are golden. When the cakes are cooked they will spring back when lightly pressed. Turn the cakes onto a wire rack to cool. Stick the cakes together with jam and cream. Sprinkle the top with confectioners' sugar.

Chocolate Fudge Triangles

PREPARATION TIME: 25 minutes

COOKING TIME: 30 minutes for base, 10 minutes for topping

OVEN TEMPERATURE: 350°F

A stick of butter
¼ cup superfine sugar
1½ cups all-purpose flour

Fudge Topping
A stick of butter
¼ cup superfine sugar
2 tblsp corn syrup
⅔ cup condensed milk
4oz plain chocolate

Cream the butter and sugar together until fluffy. Add the flour and stir until the mixture binds. Knead until smooth. Roll out and press into a shallow 8 inch square pan. Prick with a fork and bake in the oven for 30 minutes. Cool in the pan. Put the ingredients for the topping in a heavy saucepan and stir until dissolved. Slowly boil and stir for 7 minutes. Cool the

topping a little and spread over the cooky base. Leave it to set. When set, cut into squares, then cut diagonally to make triangles.

Lemon July Cake

PREPARATION TIME: 30 minutes

COOKING TIME: 25 minutes

OVEN TEMPERATURE: 375°F

Base
A stick of butter or margarine
½ cup sugar
1 egg, beaten
1½ cups flour
2 tsp baking powder

1st Topping
⅔ cup water
3 tblsp sugar
1 tblsp cornstarch
Juice of two lemons

2nd Topping
⅔ cup milk
1 tsp cornstarch
2 tblsp butter
6 tblsp sugar
Shredded coconut to sprinkle

Base
Cream the butter and sugar, add the egg and flour and pour into a pan and press down. Bake in the oven for 20 minutes.

1st Topping
Mix the water with the cornstarch to make a paste. Boil with the other ingredients until the mixture begins to thicken, stirring constantly. Spread on the cooked cake base while the mixture is still warm.

2nd Topping
Boil milk and cornstarch until it thickens. Add the the butter and sugar, creamed. Mix well and spread on top of the July. Sprinkle with the shredded coconut, cut into fingers and serve.

This page: Chocolate Brownies (top), Chocolate Fudge Triangles (bottom) and Flapjacks (center).

Facing page: Victoria Sponge (top right), Lemon July Cake (center left) and Coconut Specials (bottom).

Chocolate Brownies

PREPARATION TIME: 25 minutes

COOKING TIME: 35 minutes

OVEN TEMPERATURE: 350°F

1 cup all-purpose flour
½ tsp baking powder
4oz plain chocolate
¼ cup butter
½ cup soft brown sugar
2 eggs
6 tblsp walnuts
6 tblsp mixed fruit

Frosting
4oz plain chocolate
1 tblsp butter

Sift the flour and baking powder together in a bowl. Melt the chocolate in a bowl over a small saucepan of hot water. Cream the butter for the brownies with the sugar until light and fluffy. Beat in the eggs separately, adding the flour with the second egg. Beat the melted chocolate into the mixture, then fold in the walnuts and fruit. Grease and line a shallow 8 inch square pan and bake in the oven for 35 minutes. Cut into squares while still warm and cool in the pan.

Spiced Cookies

PREPARATION TIME: 20 minutes

COOKING TIME: 15 minutes

OVEN TEMPERATURE: 350°F

1 cup wholewheat flour
½ tsp bicarbonate of soda
1 tsp ground cinnamon
1 tsp mixed spice
¼ cup rolled oats
6 tblsp sugar
6 tblsp butter or margarine
1 tblsp corn syrup
1 tblsp milk

Put the flour, bicarbonate of soda, cinnamon, mixed spice, oats and sugar into a bowl. Melt the butter in a small saucepan with the syrup and milk. Pour the liquid into the dry ingredients and beat until smooth. Make the mixture into little balls and place them a little apart on a lightly-greased cooky sheet. Flatten each one. Bake in the oven for 15 minutes until golden, and cool on the cooky sheet.

Macaroons

PREPARATION TIME: 20 minutes

COOKING TIME: 20 minutes

OVEN TEMPERATURE: 350°F

1 cup superfine sugar
10 tblsp ground almonds
1 tblsp rice flour
2 egg whites
Rice paper
20 split almonds

Mix the sugar, almonds and rice flour together. In a separate bowl, beat the egg whites lightly and add the ready-mixed dry ingredients. Let the mixture stand for 5 minutes. Line a cooky sheet with rice paper. Mold the mixture into little balls and place them on the lined cooky sheet slightly apart. Gently flatten the macaroons and put an almond on each one. Bake in the oven for 20 minutes, then cool on cooky sheet. Makes 20.

Almond Slices

PREPARATION TIME: 20 minutes

COOKING TIME: 20 minutes

OVEN TEMPERATURE: 400°F

Pastry Base
2 cups all-purpose flour
½ cup butter
¼ tsp salt
Cold water to mix

Topping
4 tblsp jam
½ cup sugar
½ cup confectioners' sugar
¾ cup ground almonds
1 egg, plus 1 egg white
A few drops almond essence
2 tblsp flaked almonds to decorate

Chocolate Frosting

6oz plain chocolate
2 tblsp light cream

To Decorate

1 packet chocolate chips
6 tblsp whole nuts

Sift together the dry ingredients into a bowl and make a well in the center. Add the sugar, syrup, eggs, oil and milk and beat until smooth. Grease and line a 9 inch cake pan and pour in the cake mixture. Cook in the oven for 45-50 minutes; leave in the pan for a few minutes before turning out the cake onto a wire rack.

To Make the Chocolate Frosting

Put the chocolate and cream into a small, heavy pan and heat gently until melted. Cool the mixture slightly and pour over the cake. Decorate with chocolate chips, or nuts.

Harvest Crunchies

PREPARATION TIME: 20 minutes

COOKING TIME: 15 minutes

OVEN TEMPERATURE: 375°F

¾ cup all-purpose flour
½ tsp mixed spice
¾ cup wholewheat flour
2 tblsp oatmeal
½ cup butter or margarine
¼ cup soft brown sugar
2 tblsp white raisins
2 tblsp milk

Sift the flour and spice into a bowl. Stir in the wholewheat flour and oatmeal. Cut the fat into the mixture until it resembles a stiff dough by adding the milk. Flour a work surface and turn the dough out onto it. Lightly knead the dough and roll it out until very thin. With a 3 inch fluted cooky cutter, cut out rounds and place them on a lightly-greased cooky sheet. Bake in the oven, then cool on a wire rack. Makes 20.

Sift the flour and salt into a bowl and cut in the butter until it resembles fine breadcrumbs. Add enough water to mix into a pliable dough. Roll out the dough onto a floured surface and use to line a greased or dampened shallow 10x6 inch baking pan. Pinch the long edges to form a border. Cover the base with jam. In a clean bowl, mix together the sugars and almonds. Beat well and then add the whole egg, egg white and almond essence. Use the almond mixture to cover the jam, spreading evenly with a knife. Sprinkle with almonds. Bake in the oven for 20 minutes until well risen and golden. When cooked, cut in the pan and leave to cool for 10 minutes. Then remove from pan and leave to finish cooling on a wire rack.

Viennese Fingers

PREPARATION TIME: 20 minutes

COOKING TIME: 15 minutes

OVEN TEMPERATURE: 350°F

¾ cup butter or margarine
¼ cup confectioners' sugar
Grated rind of 1 orange
1 cup all-purpose flour
6 tblsp cornstarch

Cream together the butter, sugar and orange rind until fluffy. Sieve the flour and cornstarch together and beat well into the mixture. Fill a pastry bag fitted with a 1 inch fluted tip and pipe 3 inch fingers, well separated, onto a sheet of non-stick silicone paper. Bake in the oven for 15 minutes and, when cooked, transfer to a wire rack to cool. If required, two fingers can be sandwiched together with a little apricot jam. Makes 12.

Chocolate Fudge Cake

PREPARATION TIME: 15 minutes

COOKING TIME: 45-50 minutes

OVEN TEMPERATURE: 325°F

1¾ cups all-purpose flour
1 tsp bicarbonate of soda
1 tsp baking powder
2 tblsp cocoa powder
10 tblsp soft brown sugar
2 tblsp corn syrup
2 eggs
¾ cup oil
1¼ cups milk

Facing page: Macaroons (top), Spiced Cookies (right) and Harvest Crunchies (bottom left). This page: Chocolate Fudge Cake (top), Viennese Fingers (left) and Almond Slices (bottom).

Celebration Cakes

round the bottom of the cake. With a medium, plain tip make bulbs between each of the stars on the inner edge of the cake. Make another row of bulbs on the side of the cake above the stars. Colour a little of the frosting pink and fit a pastry bag with a writing tip. Make a row of dropped loops from each of the bulbs on the top of the cake. From the point of alternate stars on the top edge of the cake make a row of dropped loops. Go round the cake again making loops on the stars omitted on the first round. Make a bulb on the point of each of the stars. With the pink frosting, make a scallop on the cake board round the stars. Write the message with swirls round it in the shape of 'S's and 'C's on the top of the cake and place the flowers, a little fern and the ribbon in position.

Boy's Birthday Cake

8 inch square, rich fruit cake
Recipe apricot glaze
1¾lb almond paste
Royal frosting, made with 3lb
*   confectioners' sugar*
Food coloring – blue
8 silver leaves for the top
16 silver leaves for the side panels

Brush the top of the cake with the apricot glaze. Cover the cake with the almond paste and leave it to dry. Attach the cake to the board with a little frosting. Flat frost the sides and top of the cake and let it dry. Fit a pastry bag with a large tip and make a continuous 'S' pattern on the top edge and the base of the cake. Make 4 bars horizontally across and down the corners of the cake. At each of the 4 corners, and

Mother's Day Cake

7 or 8 inch square or round cake
Recipe apricot glaze
1½lb almond paste
Royal frosting, made with 2lb
*   confectioners' sugar*
Food colorings – green, yellow
Green ribbon
Frosted flowers

Brush the top and sides of the cake with apricot glaze and cover with almond paste; leave to dry. With a little frosting, attach the cake to the cake board and flat frost the top and sides; leave to dry. Using a pastry bag fitted with a leaf tip, make a row of leaves in white frosting facing outwards around the bottom of the cake. Then make an overlapping circle of white leaves around the top edge of the cake. Fill another pastry bag with green-colored frosting and make a row of leaves facing outwards on top. Finally, make an overlapping circle of green leaves on the top. Fill a pastry bag with a little yellow-colored frosting and fit a medium writing tip and write 'Mother' on the top surface of the cake. Attach the frosted flowers on the top surface with a dab of frosting and, using the pastry bag with green frosting and the leaf tip again, make a few leaves around the flowers to finish. Decorate with the green ribbon.

Girl's Birthday Cake

8 inch round, rich fruit cake
Recipe apricot glaze
1¾lb almond paste
Royal frosting, made with 3lb
*   confectioners' sugar*
3 frosted flowers
Food coloring – pink
Pink ribbon
Frond of asparagus fern

Brush the top and sides of the cake with apricot glaze. Cover the cake with the almond paste. Attach the cake to the board with a little frosting. Flat frost the top and the sides of the cake. Fit a pastry bag with a large star tip and make a circle of stars round the top edge of the cake. Make a row of stars

This page: Girl's Birthday Cake and Boy's Birthday Cake.

Facing page: Mother's Day Cake.

on the top of the cake, make a single line from the flat surface of the cake crossing the continuous 'S' and ending in the corner. Fit a small star tip and frost vertically down the corners of the cake, covering the ends of the bars. Frost the decorative lines on the top of the cake, starting with a long line with a dot at each end and working out and down with shorter lines towards the outer edge. Write the name in the center of the cake. Color a little of the frosting blue and fit a writing tip onto the pastry bag. Make 2 rows of scallops on the top edge of the cake, a row on each side of the continuous 'S', ending at the corner where the corner bars start. Go over the name in blue. Make a dropped loop round the base of the cake, with the point of the loops at each of the corners. Attach 2 silver leaves at the base corners of each of the 4 side panels, and 2 silver leaves on the top of the cake at each of the 4 corners attached to the flat surface of the cake.

Silver Wedding Anniversary Cake

8 or 9 inch square, rich fruit cake
Recipe apricot glaze
1¾-2lb almond paste
Royal frosting, made with 2½lb
  confectioners' sugar
8 silver leaves
Silver non-toxic coloring

Brush the top and the sides of the cake with apricot glaze and cover with almond paste. Leave the cake to dry. Attach the cake to the board with a little frosting. Flat frost the top and sides of the cake, giving 2 or 3 coats. Fit your pastry bag with a medium writing tip. Using a saucepan lid or a round template, draw a circle in the center of the top of the cake. Using a medium-sized five-star tip, pipe a continuous swirl round the bottom edge of the cake and finish off each corner with a shell. With a smaller star tip, pipe a small dot on the top edge of the cake in the center of the top edge of each of the side panels and divide the space between the original dot and the corner of the cake with a further

It is most important that a celebration cake should feed the desired number of guests, so here is a guide:

Round	Square	Portions
6 inch	5 inch	20-30
7½-8 inch	7 inch	40-45
10 inch	9 inch	70-80
11 inch	10 inch	100-110
12 inch	12 inch	130-140

NB: for decorating simple cakes, candies can be utilised and are easily applied to butter frosting. These are much used in novelty cake designs.

dot. You should have 3 dots on each of the top sides of the cake. Using these as a guide, join them together by making a scallop, with the dots marking the points of the scallop. Using a writing tip, pipe with a scribbling line between the scallop on the sides of the cake and the template circle drawn on the top of the cake. The scribbling should be done with a continuous line that never crosses itself. Using the same tip, overfrost the template-drawn circle with a continuously twisting line. On the side panels and on the corners of the cake, create three beads in

descending size below each of the points of the scallop. Overfrost the continuous swirls round the bottom of the cake with a plain, continuous swirl beginning and ending with an 'S' shape. Make the '25' in the circle on top of the cake, then – when dry – overfrost this again with white. Fit your pastry bag with a medium star tip and, having positioned the silver leaves, secure them with a frosted rosette. Using a fine paintbrush, gently paint the continuous swirl overfrost on the circle on the top surface of the cake and also the top of the '25' with a single silver line.

Silver Wedding Anniversary Cake.

Golden Wedding Cake

10 inch)round, rich fruit cake
Recipe apricot glaze
2¼lb almond paste
Royal frosting, made from 3lb
*   confectioners' sugar*
Food coloring – yellow
6 gold leaves
Yellow ribbon

Brush the sides and top of the cake with the apricot glaze. Cover the cake with the almond paste and leave to dry. Attach the cake to the board with a little frosting. Flat frost the top and sides of the cake. Fit a pastry bag with a large star tip and make a row of shells round the top of the cake. Create a row of shells round the bottom of the cake. Fit the pastry bag with a smaller star tip and create continuous 'C's on the shells on the top of the cake. Fit the pastry bag with a medium-sized plain tip and make a scallop on the top of the cake round the shells. Round the bottom of the cake, on the board, make a scallop round the shells. Repeat the scallop on the side of the cake under the shells on the top edge of the cake. Colour a little of the frosting yellow and, using a writing tip, repeat the pattern of continuous 'C's on the top edge of the cake. Make a dropped loop on top of the shell at the base of the cake. Fit the same pastry bag with a leaf tip and make inverted leaves between the shells at the base of the cake, with the point of the leaves creeping up the sides of the cake. With a writing tip, write the words and surround them with 'S's and 'C's. Decorate with a real rose or any other flower, or frosted flowers and/or gold leaves.

Diana Wedding Cake

Two-Tier Round Cake
10 inch round, rich fruit cake
6 or 7 inch round, rich fruit cake
2 x recipe apricot glaze
3lb almond paste
Royal frosting, made from 3½lb
*   confectioners' sugar*
Silver cake boards: 13 inch and 8 or
*   9 inch*
32 silver leaves
8 frosted flowers
4 round pillars

Brush the top and sides of the cake with apricot glaze and cover with almond paste. Leave the cake to dry. Attach the cake to the board

with a little frosting. Flat frost the top and sides of the cake, giving three coats and an extra coat on the base cake. Fit a pastry bag with a large star tip and make shells round the bottom of each of the cakes. Using the same tip, mark the cake surface lightly at the edge as though it were square – treat it as though it had four corners, putting a dab of frosting in each of the four corners and a smaller dab at the center of each of the four sides. From each of the dabs which mark the center of the sides make an inverted 'S', finishing at the corner

mark. Repeat this from where you started and mirror the original shape towards the other corner point. Repeat this round the cake. Make a 'C' facing the center of the cake, with its back marking the center point of the side. Overpipe all the decorative swirls, the 'S's and 'C's twice. Fit a pastry bag with a medium-sized plain tip and make a continuously twisting scallop on the upper edge of the sides of the cakes. Repeat this pattern on the cake board around the shells. With the same tip, frost over the decorative swirls, 'S's and 'C's on

the tops of the cakes. Make a scallop on the top surface of the cake, encompassing the 'C's in the curves; three curves to each imaginary side. Make dropped loops under the continuously twisting scallop on the sides of

This page: Golden Wedding Cake. Facing page: Diana Wedding Cake.

Lindsey Jane
Wedding Cake.

cakes. On the sides of the cake below the loops, attach the flowers and leaves with a little frosting, four flowers per cake below each 'C' and a frosting rosette to attach the other leaves between each of the flowers. Assemble the cake using the pillars and decorate the top with flowers.

Lindsey Jane Wedding Cake

Two-Tier Square Cake
6 inch square, rich fruit cake
10 inch square, rich fruit cake
2 x recipe apricot glaze
3¼lb almond paste
Royal frosting made with 4lb
* confectioners' sugar*
28 pink frosted roses, to decorate
Asparagus fern, to decorate
Silver cake boards, 8 inch and 12
* inch*
4 square pillars
2 narrow ribbon bows

This design is suitable for a 1, 2 or 3-tier cake. The roses are chosen to match the bridal attire.
Brush the sides and tops of the cakes with apricot glaze and cover with almond paste. Leave to dry. Attach the cakes to the cake boards with a dab of frosting. Flat frost the cakes, giving two or three coats all over. Fit a pastry bag with a medium-sized shell tip and decorate shells on the top edge of the cakes, the bottom edge and up each of the corners. Apply with frosting on the top of the cakes in each corner 2 shells facing each other. Fit the pastry bag with a medium-sized plain tip and create a shallow scallop round the top side of the cake. Create an 'S'-shaped swirl, filling each of the small scallops. On the bottom tier, put a cluster of roses in the middle of the cake, surrounded by fern, two roses in each of the corners and one rose at the base of each of the corners. On the top tier, repeat but with a single rose at the top of each corner and the ribbon bows on top of the cake. Assemble the cake using the pillars.

Christening Cake

8 inch round, rich fruit cake
Recipe apricot glaze
1¾lb almond paste
Royal frosting, made with 3lb
* confectioners' sugar*
Food coloring – blue
½oz almond paste
1 narrow, white ribbon bow

Brush the top and sides of the cake with the apricot glaze. Cover the cake with the almond paste and leave it to dry. Attach the cake to the board with a little frosting. Flat frost the top and sides of the cake with the royal frosting. Fit a pastry bag with a large star tip. With a frosting comb, comb the sides of the cake with a swirling line and make a row of shells round the top of the cake. Fit a pastry bag with a small star tip and make a scallop round the top of the shells. Make a graduated rope round the bottom of the cake with a large, dropped loop round the rope. Fit the pastry bag with a small plain tip and make a scallop on the top of the cake next to the shells. Write the name of the baby on the top of the cake. Color a little royal frosting blue. Using a writing tip, make beads at the points of each of the tips. Make another scallop onto the silver board. Go over the name with the blue, making small 'C's and scrolls. To make the bootees, color a little molding frosting pale blue and shape two. Press a small hole towards the end of each of the oval shapes. With a writing tip, pipe round the holes, making a little bow at the front. Decorate with a silver ball and put the small bow between the bootees.

Tracy Rose Wedding Cake

Three-Tier Square
5 inch square, rich fruit cake
8 inch square, rich fruit cake
11 inch square, rich fruit cake
3 x recipe apricot glaze
5lb almond paste
Royal frosting, made with 8lb
  confectioners' sugar
2 x recipe molding frosting, peach
  color (to make 60 molded roses)
3 cake boards: 7 inch, 10 inch and 14
  inch
Food colorings – green, peach (brown)
8 square cake pillars
2 rectangular silver boards

Brush the top and sides of the cakes with apricot glaze and cover with almond paste; leave to dry. Attach the cakes to the silver cake boards with a dab of frosting. Flat frost the tops of the cakes with the peach colored royal frosting. Cut the thin, rectangular cake boards lengthways down the middle and then cut each widthways with a sharp knife. Cut the corners off each piece diagonally so that they will go together to form a square with a square hole in the center. Place each on a sheet of wax paper and flat frost onto the white side with a palette knife; leave to dry. Fit a pastry bag with a medium writing tip and the other with a basket weave tip. Hold the basket weave tip sideways and on the side of the first cake pipe 3 lines, evenly spaced, one above the other and all of the same length. Pipe a vertical line using the writing tip along the edge of the basket weaving. Continue this process until the cake is covered. Repeat the basket weave method on each of the cardboard lids. To make the molded flowers see chapter on decorations. Color a little of the royal frosting green and fit a pastry bag with a leaf tip. Color a little more royal frosting a dark peach and use it to fill a bag fitted with a star tip. Continue to use the writing tip filled with the tinted peach royal frosting as used in the basket weave. Position the molded frosting roses facing outward round the top edges of the 2 bottom tiers and in a radiating pattern on the small top tier. Make frosted dark peach stars between each of the roses and dot the center of each star using the tinted peach royal frosting. Make frosted leaves at random round the flowers. Place the pillars on a tray and frost small stars dotted with tinted peach for the center of the flower. Again, frost leaves at random and leave to dry.

To Assemble the Cake
Place the basket lids round the outer edge of each of the cake's bottom two tiers and, with a little frosting, secure them to the top of the cake. Make sure that there is enough room in the square at the center of each cake for the four pillars.
Note: the cake board can be frosted with a palette knife to surround each of the cakes, if required.

This page: Christening Cake.

Facing page: Tracy Rose Wedding Cake.

and, with inverted 'S's and 'C's, pipe little swirls around the words. Create the starbursts round the cross. Decorate with the ribbon.

Fiona Anne Wedding Cake

Three-Tier Round
6 inch round, rich fruit cake
8 inch round, rich fruit cake
10 inch round, rich fruit cake
3 x recipe apricot glaze
4lb almond paste
Royal frosting, made with 7lb
  confectioners' sugar
60 silver leaves
30 frosted sugar roses, painted with
  non-toxic silver food coloring
Silver cake boards: 8 inch, 10 inch
  and 13 inch
8 round cake pillars

Brush the top and the sides of the cake with apricot glaze, cover with almond paste and leave to dry. Attach the cakes to the cake boards with a dab of frosting. Flat frost the cakes, giving three coats all over and an extra coat for the tops. Fit a pastry bag with a large star tip and create inverted shells with the tail of the shell going up the side of the cake. With the same tip, create 'C's round the top edge of each of the cakes and leave to dry. Pipe a further 'C' on top of the first. Fit the pastry bag with a medium plain tip and create a further 'C' on top of the original two. Working along the side edge of the cakes, pipe a dropped loop with a swirling action to create a graduated rope. With a plain writing tip, create a dropped loop round the tail of each of the base shells, missing out a shell as you pipe. When you have gone round the cake, repeat the process, crossing the dropped loop from the tail of the shell that you missed out on the first round. On the tops of the cakes, create a scallop round each of the 'C' shapes. Fit the pastry bag with the medium plain tip and create a bead to conceal the tail of each of the base shells.

Confirmation Cake

8 or 9 inch square, rich fruit cake
Recipe apricot glaze
1¾-2lb almond paste
Royal frosting, made with 2½lb
  confectioners' sugar
Food coloring – violet
Violet ribbon

Brush the top and the sides of the cake with apricot glaze and cover with almond paste. Leave the cake to dry. Attach the cake to the board with a little frosting. Flat frost the top and the sides of the cake, giving 2 or 3 coats. Fit a pastry bag with a medium-sized 5-point tip and make a row of graduated ropes round the top edge of the cake. To do this, start from the center of one side and mark with a small dot of frosting. Divide the area between the corners of the cake and the original dot with another dot and work your way round each of the sides of the cake. You now have 3 dots on each side of the cake. Frost between each of the dots in a continuous swirl which gets thicker at the halfway mark and decreases in size towards the end. Repeat the graduated ropes round the bottom edge of the cake. Fit the pastry bag with a smaller star tip and make a scallop round each of the graduated ropes. You should have 4 on each side of the cake on both the top edge and the bottom. On the flat surface of the cake, make a scallop using the same tip as before, but facing outwards, so you have concave and convex scallops on the top edge of the cake. Fit the pastry bag with a plain writing tip and go over the first scallop with a continuously twisting line. Fit another pastry bag with a little violet-colored frosting and, towards one side of the top of the cake, make the outer line of the cross with a continuous line. Take a little white frosting and thin it with a small amount of lemon juice until it flows. When the violet-colored outline of the cross is dry, flood the shape with the liquid icing. Burst any bubbles and leave it to dry. With the violet icing and writing tip, write the words 'God Bless'

This page: Confirmation Cake.

Facing page: Fiona Anne Wedding Cake.

Reserve 15 roses for the bottom cake, 10 for the middle tier and 5 for the top tier. Reserve 30 silver leaves for the bottom cake, 20 for the middle tier and 10 for the top tier. Space the decorations as follows: 1 rose, with twinned silver leaves on either side, with a frosted forget-me-not (using a forget-me-not tip) to secure the leaves and a single rose placed slightly lower down on the side of the cake, followed by another rose and surrounded by twin silver leaves. Assemble the cake using the pillars and decorate the top with flowers.

Valentine Cake

8 or 9 inch round, rich fruit cake, cut to a heart shape
Recipe apricot glaze
1½lb almond paste
Royal frosting, made with 3lb confectioners' sugar
Red and cream molded roses
Food coloring – green
Red ribbon

Brush the top and sides of the cake with apricot glaze and cover with almond paste; leave to dry. With a little frosting, attach the cake to the cake board and flat frost the top and sides; leave to dry. Make two rows of shells around the base of the cake in white frosting. Attach the red and cream molded roses with a dab of frosting on the top surface of the cake. Colour a little frosting with the green food coloring and, using a leaf tip, make a few leaves round the molded roses. Make a bow with the red ribbon and attach to the top surface of the cake to finish.

Good Luck Cake

8 inch round, rich fruit cake
Recipe apricot glaze
1¾lb almond paste
Royal frosting, made with 2lb confectioners' sugar
Food colorings – violet, pink
1oz black molding frosting
2 silver leaves
1 silver horseshoe, small
1 narrow, black bow

Brush the top and the sides of the cake with the apricot glaze. Cover the cake with the almond paste and let it dry. Flat frost the top and sides of the cake, having first

attached the cake to the board with a little frosting. With a small star tip, make a row of shells round the top edge of the cake. Create a row of graduated ropes round the top edge of the side of the cake. Using the same tip, make a double row of shells round the bottom of the cake. Color a little frosting pink and, with a writing tip, make a loose scallop round the inside edge of the cake on the top surface. Make frosted dropped loops over the 2 rows of shells at the bottom of the cake. Color a little frosting violet and, with a writing tip, make a scallop pattern round the outer edge of the top of the cake. Repeat the pattern on the board round the cake. Make a small bulb on the side of the cake on the point of the pink dropped loops. Write the words 'Good Luck' or 'Best Wishes' on the top of the cake using a writing tip and violet-colored frosting. With the pink frosting, pipe a line under the words and pipe a bulb at the point of the violet dropped loops. Roll out the black molding frosting and either cut out the shape of a cat, using a sharp knife, or draw the cat onto a piece of greaseproof paper and use it as a guide. When the cat has been cut out, let it dry and put it in place with a little frosting. Arrange the leaves and the ribbon.

21st Birthday Cake

This design can also be used for a golden wedding or silver wedding anniversary cake. Just omit the '21' and change the color used: either yellow balls for a golden wedding or silver balls for a silver wedding, writing your message on the top of the cake.

8 or 9 inch square, rich fruit cake
Recipe apricot glaze
1¾-2lb almond paste
Royal frosting, made with 2½lb confectioners' sugar
Food coloring – violet
4 medium-sized silver horseshoes

Brush the sides and top of the cake with apricot glaze. Cover the cake with the almond paste and leave to dry. Attach the cake to the board with a little frosting. Flat frost the top and the sides of the cake. When the frosting is dry, make a template. Alternatively, draw a circle round a small saucepan lid or fluted jelly mold, onto a piece of wax paper. Use either of these templates to mark out the top of

the cake. Fit a pastry bag with a large star tip and make shells round the base of the cake. Using a plain writing tip filled with white frosting, mark a point 1 inch from the top edge of the cake on each of the side panels. Make a further point halfway between the first mark and the corner of the cake. You will now have 3 dots on each of the side panels. Use them as a guide to enable you to make inverted scallops. The dots mark the points of each scallop and also the corner of the cake. Using your template and the same tip, make the decorative shape on the top surface of the cake. Fit your pastry bag with a forget-me-not tip. Make random forget-me-nots between the scallop on the side of the cake and the template-drawn pattern on the top. Fit the pastry bag with a medium, plain writing tip and make an inner circle on the flat surface of the cake echoing the shape drawn with the use of the template. Write the figures '21' and the name, if required. Color a little of the frosting violet and, using a medium tip, dot the center of each flower. Using the violet frosting make a scallop shape on the cake board, curving round each of the shells. Using a small writing tip, go over the original template-drawn line with a continuously twisting line. Go over the '21' and the name with the violet frosting. This can be done with half straight and half continuous twists. Using a little white frosting, attach the horseshoes in the center of each of the side panels of the cake.

Flower Birthday Cake

7 inch or 8 inch round, rich fruit cake or Madeira cake
Recipe apricot glaze
1½lb almond paste
Recipe pink molding frosting
Selection of molded flowers
Ribbon – color of your choice

Brush the top and sides of the cake with apricot glaze and cover with almond paste; leave to dry. With a little frosting, attach the cake to the cake board and cover with the pink molding frosting; leave to dry. Attach the molded flowers with a dab of frosting. Decorate with the ribbon.

Engagement Cake

8 or 9 inch square, rich fruit cake
Recipe apricot glaze
1¾-2lb almond paste
Royal frosting, made with 2½lb
  confectioners' sugar
Three frosted flowers
Food colorings – pink, blue
Pink ribbon

Brush the cake with the apricot glaze. Cover the cake with the almond paste and let it dry. Attach the cake to the board with a little frosting. Flat frost the top and the sides of the cake. Fit a pastry bag with a medium star tip and make shells round the base of the cake. Using the same tip, make 'C's at the corners of the cake on the top surface of the cake. Pipe another 'C' on top of the first. On the edge of the top of the cake, create a continuous 'S' pattern and repeat it on the top of the first row. With the same tip, make a line on the flat surface of the cake. Using a writing tip, make another line on the inside of the first line. Color some of the frosting blue and, with a writing tip, make another line round the top edge of the cake. Go over over the 'C's in the corners of the cake and make dropped loops over the shells at the bottom of the cake. Fit another pastry bag with a medium-sized plain tip. Color a little icing pink and use it to make continuous loops, starting and ending with an 'S'. Write the message on the top of the cake and make bulbs between each of the shells where each of the blue loops point. With the blue frosting, make – using a writing tip – small, decorative, inverted 'C' and 'S' shapes round the message. Attach the frosted flowers and the ribbon.

This page: 21st Birthday Cake.

Facing page: Valentine Cake and Engagement Cake.

Easter and Christmas Cakes

Special cakes are traditionally used for the celebration of religious festivals; the most popular being the traditional Christmas cake and the simnel cake at Easter. Not everybody enjoys rich cake, so there are sponge variations in this book for both Easter and Christmas.

Simnel Cake

PREPARATION TIME: 40 minutes

COOKING TIME: 3 hours

OVEN TEMPERATURE: 325°F reduced to 300°F

8 inch round, rich fruit cake mixture
1¾lb almond paste
2 tblsp apricot glaze
1 egg white, beaten
Ribbon to decorate

Place half the mixture in a prepared, deep cake pan. Roll out a quarter of the almond paste into a 8 inch circle and lay it on top of the mixture. Spread the remaining mixture on the top of the almond paste. Bake in the oven for 1 hour, lower the temperature and bake for a further 2½ hours. Leave in the pan for 5 minutes and turn onto a wire rack to cool. Roll out a third of the remaining almond paste into a 8 inch circle. Brush the top of the cake with apricot glaze. Press the almond paste circle on top of the cake and brush with beaten egg white. Shape the remaining almond paste into balls and place round the edge. Brown under a hot broiler and allow to cool. Decorate with ribbon.

Daffodil Cake

9 inch round Madeira cake
Recipe vanilla-flavored butter frosting
Molding frosting daffodil
3 tblsp apricot jam
1 tblsp cocoa powder

Slice the cake and spread with the jam. Use half of the butter frosting and sandwich the cake together. Spread the top of the cake with a ¼ of the remaining butter frosting. Smooth it with a palette knife. Fill a pastry bag with the remaining butter frosting and fit it with a 5-point star tip. Make shells round the edge of the cake. Put the daffodil on the cake. Mix a little butter frosting with cocoa powder. With a pastry bag fitted with a writing tip, write 'Easter' on the cake below the daffodil.

Easter Nest

8 inch round lemon sponge (beaten or Victoria)
1 box orange-flavored chocolate sticks
½ cup candy-coated chocolate speckled eggs
Recipe lemon-flavored butter frosting

Put the cake on a plate or cake board. Cover the cake with lemon-flavored butter frosting. Put a

This page: Daffodil Cake (top) and Simnel Cake (bottom).

Facing page: Easter Cake with Chicks (top) and Easter Nest (bottom).

ribbon round the side of the cake and make a bow. Lay the orange-flavored chocolate sticks at angles round the sides of the cake, leaving an uncovered area in the center of the cake. Fill the center with eggs.

Fruit Easter Cake with Chicks

PREPARATION TIME: 45 minutes

COOKING TIME: 1 hour 30 minutes to 1 hour 45 minutes

OVEN TEMPERATURE: 325°F

¼ cup butter
¼ cup sugar
3 eggs
1 cup flour
¾ cup mixed dried fruit
1¼ cups cake flour
1½ tsp baking powder
¼ cup chopped mixed candied fruit
¼ cup candied cherries, halved
Grated rind of 1 orange
5 tblsp orange juice
1 crushed sugar cube

To Decorate
Fluffy chicks
Yellow ribbon

Cream the butter and sugar together until light and fluffy. Beat in the eggs singly, adding a little flour after each. Toss the fruit in the remaining flour and add to the mixture with the orange rind and juice. Grease and line a 7 inch cake pan. Fill with the mixture and smooth with the back of a spoon. Sprinkle with some of the crushed sugar cube. Bake in the oven for 1½-1¾ hours. Turn out and cool on a wire rack. Decorate with yellow ribbon, chicks and fresh or artificial flowers. Sprinkle top of cake with remaining sugar cube.

Festive Garland

If you prefer you can make edible decorations for this cake.

8 inch quick mix cake, baked in a ring mold
Recipe apricot glaze
Recipe butter frosting
1 round cake board
Holly leaves, berries, Christmas roses, mistletoe, candle and ribbon (color of your choice)

Split the cake and sandwich together with the glaze. Put the cake on the plate or cake board and cover with the frosting, peaking it as you go around. Press the roses, holly leaves, berries and mistletoe into the cake, leaving a gap for the bow. When the frosting is dry and hard, place a candle in the center of the ring and attach the bow in the space reserved.

Christmas Bells

7 inch or 8 inch square Christmas cake
Royal frosting, made with 2½lb confectioners' sugar
½ recipe white molding frosting
½ cup granulated sugar
4 sprigs of holly, real or artificial
1 yard narrow, white satin ribbon
Food coloring – pink

Put the cake on a silver cake board. Royal frost the cake and leave to dry between coats. Roll out the molding frosting and, using a bell shape cutter, cut 10 bells and leave them to dry on non-stick silicone paper. Mix the granulated sugar and pink food color well until the sugar becomes pink. Sprinkle over the bells and leave to dry. Fill a pastry bag, fitted with a medium-sized star tip, with the royal frosting. Make a row of shells round the bottom of the cake. Make a border of shells round the top of the cake and a line of shells up each of the 4 corners of the cake and allow the frosting to dry. Make 5 bows with the narrow, white ribbon. With a little frosting sugar secure two frosting bells on each side panel of the cake. The tops of the bells should be nearest to each of the 4 corners. Two of the bells should be placed in the center of the top of the cake, with the tops of the bells together. Put a ribbon bow above each of the bells. Position the sprigs of holly in each of the four corners on top of the cake.

Christmas Tree

8 inch square quick mix cake or rich fruit cake mix
Recipe apricot glaze
Recipe almond paste, if using fruit cake
Recipe butter frosting, if using quick mix cake
1lb molding frosting

To Decorate
1 cake board
Silver balls
Shredded coconut to sprinkle
Recipe royal frosting

8oz molding frosting, white
Chocolate sticks
Gold or silver non-toxic food coloring
Food coloring – red, blue, green, yellow
8oz molding frosting

Cut the cake diagonally and place the outer edges of the square next to one another, i.e. back-to-back to produce a triangular shape. If using a fruit cake, brush with apricot glaze and cover with almond paste. If using a butter frosting on a quick cake mixture, cover the cake with the butter frosting and leave on the cake board. Roll out the molding frosting and, using a fluted pastry cutter, cut circles and then cut each one in half and use to stick onto the butter frosting. Start at the bottom edge of the cake and overlap slightly until you reach the top. With the remaining frosting, make some small presents and a square tub for the tree. Cover the tree trunk with a little of the remaining butter frosting and lay the chocolate sticks vertically on the tree trunk. Use any remaining frosting to frost the leaves of the tree, or make the leaves if desired. Decorate with the silver balls and sprinkle with shredded coconut. With the white frosting to decorate, color small pinches in various colors and, with the white royal frosting, make strings around the various colored shapes to make more little parcels. Roll out the remaining white frosting and cut it into a star. Color with a little non-toxic gold or silver food coloring.

Traditional Christmas Cake with Holly and Roses

7 inch round Christmas cake
Recipe apricot glaze
1½lb almond paste
Royal frosting, made with 2lb confectioners' sugar

To Decorate
Silver balls
Christmas roses
Almond paste holly leaves and berries, small snowman or Santa, if available
Ribbon

Brush the cake with apricot glaze. Cover with the almond paste and leave to dry. Flat frost the top and sides of the cake with royal frosting and leave to dry again. Use a pastry bag fitted with a 5-star tip and make shells around the top edge of the cake and then on the top,

round the sides of the cake and, finally, around the bottom edge of the cake. When dry, make a further row between the top 2 rows using the 5-star tip upright to make stars. Decorate the top of the cake with almond paste holly and frosted or molded Christmas roses and a small snowman or Father Christmas, if desired. Tie the ribbon round the cake and make a bow. Push a silver ball into the center of each of the stars.

Christmas Tree (right) and Festive Garland (below).

Frosted Mistletoe Cake

This is a quick and easy Christmas cake, which can be made either round or square. Any bought decorations can be used to complement the design.

7 inch or 8 inch square or round
  Christmas cake
Recipe apricot glaze
1½lb almond paste
2lb green molding frosting
12 mistletoe leaves and berries made
  from almond paste
2ft x 2 inch length of green ribbon
Food coloring – green

Put the cake on a silver cake board. To decorate, roll out the green molding frosting. With a small, sharp knife cut out several mistletoe leaves. Make them long and narrow with rounded ends and mark them with a knife to indicate the veins. With the uncolored molding frosting roll small, pea-sized balls of frosting to represent the berries. Use the mistletoe to decorate the top of the cake. With the ribbon, tie a large bow and attach it to the top of the cake with a little royal frosting. Fill a shaker with a little frosting sugar, or put it through a small sieve and shake it gently round the edge of the cake, dusting some of the mistletoe.

Christmas Candles

2 jam-filled jelly rolls
1lb green molding frosting
4oz white molding frosting
Recipe apricot glaze
Rectangular silver cake board
Food colorings – red, yellow, blue
Red ribbon
3 cocktail sticks

Cut one jelly roll ¾ of the way down. Brush the jelly rolls with apricot glaze. Roll out the green molding frosting and cover the jelly rolls. Stand them upright with something for support. In a small, heavy saucepan stir to dissolve half to three-quarters of the white molding frosting. Roll out the

This page: Christmas Bells Cake (top) and Traditional Christmas Cake with Holly and Roses (bottom).

Facing page: Frosted Mistletoe Cake.

remaining white frosting on a surface dusted with confectioners' sugar or cornstarch and cut out 3 flame shapes. Leave on non-stick silicone paper to dry. When dry, paint a blue dot near the bottom; surround by yellow and edge with red. Reserve to dry. Pour the liquid molding frosting over the candles in a drizzle so that it dries like wax. Stick a flame in to the top of each candle, using a cocktail stick to support them. Decorate with ribbons.

Postbox

This makes a quick and easy festive cake for those who do not like traditional Christmas cake.

1 chocolate jelly roll
8oz red molding frosting
Recipe royal frosting
Recipe apricot glaze

Roll out the molding frosting and cut out two circles to cover the ends of the jelly roll. Roll out the remaining frosting to cover the rest of the jelly roll. Brush the jelly roll with the apricot glaze and cover with molding frosting. Fit a pastry bag with a writing tip and fill with some royal frosting. Frost the detail onto the postbox and leave to dry. With the remaining frosting, spoon half on top of the postbox and the remainder at the bottom. Dust with a little confectioners' sugar.

Icicles with Holly

7 inch or 8 inch square or round, rich fruit cake
Recipe apricot glaze
1½lb almond paste
Royal frosting, made with 2lb confectioners' sugar
Blue ribbon
Almond paste holly leaves and berries

Brush the top and sides of the cake with apricot glaze and cover with almond paste; leave to dry. With a little frosting, attach the cake to the cake board and flat frost the top and sides. Leave it to dry between and after coats. Using a pastry bag fitted with a shell tip, make a circle of shells on the top edge of the cake and again round the bottom of the cake. Fit the pastry bag with

a plain or fine-band tip. Place the ribbon round the sides of the cake. Make the icicles down and over the ribbon, varying them in length and width. Fit the pastry bag with a

writing tip and go over to make smaller icicles, which should hang free of the cake. Use the remaining frosting to secure the holly in a pattern on top of the cake.

This page: Postbox and Christmas Candles. Facing page: Icicles with Holly.

Gâteaux

Minted Lime Gâteau

PREPARATION TIME: 35 minutes
COOKING TIME: 20 minutes
OVEN TEMPERATURE: 375°F

½ cup sugar
3 eggs
¾ cup cake flour
3 tblsp melted butter
Grated rind of 1 lime
Flesh of 1 lime, de-pipped

Decoration
1¼ cups heavy cream
1 fresh lime
Grated chocolate (optional)

Beat the sugar and eggs together in a basin, over a saucepan of hot water, until the mixture is thick. Sieve the flour twice and fold into the beaten mixture. Mix in the lime flesh and grated rind. Grease and flour an 8 inch cake pan and fill with the mixture. Bake in the oven for 20 minutes. Cool on a wire rack.

To Decorate
Whip the cream and spread over the gâteau, reserving a little for decorating. Fill a nylon pastry bag with the remaining cream and, using a star tip, shape rosettes to decorate the gâteau. Sprinkle the sides with chocolate, if desired, and decorate with slices of lime.

Gâteau St Honoré

PREPARATION TIME: 1 hour
30 minutes
COOKING TIME: 30 minutes
OVEN TEMPERATURE: 325°F

This is a fantasy choux pastry dessert. Also known as a croquembouche, it can be built directly onto a serving stand or onto a meringue or basic pastry base, and is a French favorite for weddings. If making the choux pastry a day in advance, the buns can be crisped by heating in a preheated oven at 350°F for 5 minutes. Cool before filling and assembling.

Black Forest Gâteau

PREPARATION TIME: 35 minutes
COOKING TIME: 40 minutes
OVEN TEMPERATURE: 375°F

3 eggs
½ cup sugar
¾ cup flour
1 tblsp cocoa powder

Filling
15oz can black cherries, pitted
1 tblsp arrowroot
2 tblsp Kirsch
1¼ cups heavy cream
Grated chocolate or chocolate flakes to decorate

Place the eggs and sugar in a basin and beat over a saucepan of hot water until thick. Remove from the heat and continue to beat until cool. Sieve the cocoa powder and flour together and gently fold into the mixture using a metal spoon. Grease and line the bottom of an 8 inch cake pan. Pour the mixture into the pan and bake in the oven for 40 minutes. Turn out and cool on a wire rack.

Filling and Decoration
Drain the juice from the cherries into a pan and blend with a little arrowroot. Bring to boil and stir until it thickens. Add the cherries to the syrup and allow to cool. Cut the cake in half and sprinkle the base with a little kirsch. Whip the cream and use it to fill a nylon pastry bag fitted with a large star tip. Shape a circle of cream into the border edge of the base cake. Fill with half the cherry mixture. Sprinkle the top of the cake with a little kirsch and place on top of the filling. Spread a little cream on the sides of the gâteau and press the grated chocolate onto it using a palette knife. Shape swirls of cream on top of the gâteau and fill the center with the remaining cherries. Sprinkle with a little chocolate.

Walnut and Banana Galette

PREPARATION TIME: 45 minutes
COOKING TIME: 25 minutes
OVEN TEMPERATURE: 350°F

½ cup butter
1½ cups flour
½ cup sugar
½ cup chopped walnuts
Grated rind of ½ lemon

Filling and Decoration
1¼ cups heavy cream

2 tblsp confectioners' sugar
4 bananas

Cream the butter, sugar and lemon rind until fluffy. Fold the flour in and knead it until you have a soft dough. Put the dough in a polythene bag and chill for ½ hour in the refrigerator. Grease and flour 3 cooky sheets and mark a 7 inch circle on each. To make the circles, use a saucepan lid as a guide. Divide the dough into 3 and place a piece of dough on each circle. Press it out until it fills the circle. Sprinkle the top of each circle with chopped walnuts and bake in the oven for 25 minutes. When cooked, allow to cool before turning onto a wire rack.

Filling and Decoration
Whip the cream and fold in the confectioners' sugar. Slice the bananas and sprinkle them with a little lemon juice, which prevents them from discoloring. Stick the layers together with some cream sprinkled with banana slices. Using a nylon pastry bag filled with the remaining cream and fitted with a large star tip, shape the decoration around the top of the galette and decorate with slices of banana. Allow the galette to stand for 30 minutes before serving.

Brandied Chestnut Roll

PREPARATION TIME: 35 minutes
COOKING TIME: 12 minutes for the base, 10 minutes for the filling
OVEN TEMPERATURE: 425°F

3 eggs
½ cup sugar
2 tblsp brandy
1 cup flour

Filling
1 tblsp sugar
1¼ cups heavy cream
1 tblsp sugar
8¾oz can chestnut purée (crème de marron)
6oz plain chocolate
1 tblsp butter
2 tblsp brandy

Beat the eggs and sugar until thick. Gently fold in the sieved flour and the brandy with a metal spoon. Line and grease (bottom only) a 9x13 inch jelly roll pan. Pour the mixture into the pan and bake in the oven for 12 minutes. Cover a clean, damp cloth with a sheet of wax paper. Sprinkle the paper with 1 tblsp sugar. Turn the cake out onto the paper and remove the

wax used to line the pan. The edges of the cake will be crisp, so trim with a sharp knife. Roll up the cake by putting a clean sheet of wax over the cake. Cool on a wire tray.

Filling
Whip the cream and sugar until stiff and stir half the cream into the chestnut purée. The chestnut purée mixture must be smooth before use. Gently unroll the cake and remove the wax paper rolled with it. Spread the chestnut cream on the inner side of the cake and re-roll. Melt the chocolate in a bowl over a pan of hot water, adding the butter and brandy. Cover the cake completely with the chocolate mixture. Mark the chocolate-coated cake with a fork when half set. Pipe the whipped cream with a large tip into whirls on top of the cake.

Ginger Ice Cream Gâteau

PREPARATION TIME: 1 hour
COOKING TIME: 25 minutes
OVEN TEMPERATURE: 325°F

Ice Cream
⅔ cup milk
1 egg
6 tblsp sugar
¼ cup green ginger wine
1¼ cups heavy cream

Almond Base
3 egg whites
10 tblsp sugar
6 tblsp cornstarch
½ cup ground almonds

Topping
⅔ cup heavy cream
4 tblsp apricot jam, sieved
3 pieces stem ginger, chopped
¼ cup whole or flaked almonds, toasted

Ice Cream
Put the milk, egg and sugar into a basin over a pan of hot water. Stir continuously until the custard mixture begins to thicken. When it will coat the back of the spoon, remove it and let it cool. Stir in the ginger wine and cream. Pour into a rigid, shallow freezer container and partially freeze. When the ice cream is partially frozen, remove from the freezer and pour into a bowl. Beat until smooth and creamy. Line an 8 inch cake pan with plastic wrap and pour in the ice cream. Return to the freezer until frozen.

Almond Base
Beat the egg whites in a clean bowl until they are stiff. Add the sugar and beat again. Gently fold in the cornstarch and ground almonds. Line the bottom of a cooky sheet. Fill a nylon pastry bag fitted with a ½ inch tip with some of the almond mixture. Spread the mixture in an 8 inch circle and smooth evenly. Bake in the oven for 25 minutes.
Place the almond base on a flat plate. Carefully lift the ice cream out of the pan and peel off the plastic wrap. Place the ice cream on the almond base.

For the Topping
Whip the cream, fold in the jam, stem ginger and almonds and spread over the ice cream.

Brandied Chestnut Roll (left), Walnut and Banana Galette (below) and Black Forest Gâteau (bottom).

Peach and Almond Gâteau

PREPARATION TIME: 60 minutes

COOKING TIME: 60 minutes for cake, 20 minutes for confectioners' custard

OVEN TEMPERATURE: 350°F

4 eggs, separated
½ cup sugar
1 cup cake flour
1¼ tsp baking powder
2 tblsp corn oil
3 tblsp boiling water
1 tsp almond essence

Filling
2 tblsp apricot jam, warmed

Confectioner's Custard
3 egg yolks
¼ cup sugar
¼ cup flour
1¼ cups milk
2 tblsp butter
1 tblsp sherry

To Decorate
1¼ cups heavy cream
¼ cup flaked almonds, toasted
14½oz can sliced peaches, drained

Grease and line an 8 inch loose-bottomed, deep cake pan. Place the egg yolks, sugar, flour, oil, water and almond essence in a bowl and beat for 2 minutes with a wooden spoon. Stiffly beat the egg whites and fold into the cake mixture using a metal spoon. Pour the mixture into a prepared pan and cook in the oven for about 60 minutes until well risen. Remove cake from pan and cool on a wire rack. Remove paper when cake is cold.

For the Confectioners' Custard
Put egg yolks in a bowl and beat until smooth and creamy. Stir in the flour and mix well. Heat the milk until hot, but not boiling, and stir into the egg mixture. Return the mixture to the pan and stir, bringing it gently to the boil. Remove from the heat and beat in the butter and the sherry. Pour into a bowl, stirring occasionally to prevent a skin forming.

Assembling the Gâteau
Cut the cake into 3 layers, placing the bottom layer on a serving plate. Spread the cake with 1 tblsp of jam and half the confectioners' custard. Place the second layer on top and spread with the remaining jam and

custard. Put the top of the cake onto the filling. Spread the cake with half the cream and arrange the peaches on the top. Fit a pastry bag with a medium star tip and shape the remaining cream to decorate the gâteau. Sprinkle on the toasted almonds.

Chocolate Torte

PREPARATION TIME: 35 minutes

COOKING TIME: 1 hour 30 minutes

OVEN TEMPERATURE: 300°F

6oz plain chocolate
1 tblsp strong black coffee
¾ cup butter
¾ cup sugar
4 eggs, separated
1¼ cups cake flour
1½ tsp baking powder

Filling and Icing
Cherry jam
6oz plain chocolate
2 tblsp strong black coffee
¾ cup confectioners' sugar
⅔ cup heavy cream or
½ cup chocolate shavings
14½oz can black cherries, pitted

Melt the chocolate and coffee over a basin of hot water. Allow it to cool. Cream the butter and sugar together until light and fluffy. Slowly beat in the egg yolks and the cooled chocolate mixture. Fold in the flour using a metal spoon. Beat the egg whites in a clean, dry bowl until stiff, then fold into the mixture. Line and grease the base of an 8 inch cake pan and bake in the oven for 1½ hours. Allow the cake to cool in the pan for 10 minutes before turning onto a wire rack. Cut the cake horizontally and stick together with the cherry jam. Melt the chocolate and coffee for the frosting in a basin over a saucepan of hot water and remove from the heat. Beat in the confectioners' sugar. Pour the chocolate frosting over the cake, working it over the sides of the cake with a palette knife. When set, decorate with either the whipped cream or chocolate shavings and drained cherries.

Avocado Cheesecake

PREPARATION TIME: 30 minutes plus chilling

Crumb Base
8oz chocolate Graham crackers
6 tblsp butter, melted

Filling
2 ripe avocado pears
½ cup cream cheese
6 tblsp sugar
Juice of ½ a lemon
Grated rind of 1 lemon
2 tsp gelatin powder
2 egg whites
⅔ cup heavy cream, whipped

Decoration
⅔ cup heavy cream, whipped

Crush the crackers into fine crumbs and stir in the melted butter. Use the mixture to line a 7½ inch springform pan. Press it down to line the base and the sides. Chill well.

For the Filling
Peel and stone the avocados and save a few slices for decoration. Put the remainder into a basin and mash well. Mix in the lemon juice and grated rind, cream cheese and sugar. Beat until smooth. Dissolve the gelatin in 2 tblsp of hot water and stir into the mixture. Beat the egg whites in a clean, dry bowl and fold into the mixture with the whipped cream. Pour onto a prepared cracker base and chill thoroughly until set.

To Decorate
Carefully remove the cheesecake from the pan. Fill a nylon pastry bag, fitted with a star tip, with the cream reserved for decoration. Decorate a border of cream round the edge of the cake. Decorate with the avocado slices.
NB: sprinkle the avocado with lemon juice to prevent it from discoloring. This is useful when reserving the slices for decoration.

This page: Chocolate Torte (top) and Apricot Meringue (bottom).

Facing page: Avocado Cheesecake (top), Ginger Ice Cream Gâteau (center left) and Peach and Almond Gâteau (bottom).

Index

Dep. Leg. B-22.751-6